D1558017

UNDERSTANDING HYDROPONICS

UNDERSTANDING HYDROPONICS

Growing Plants Without Soil

By George Sullivan

FREDERICK WARNE   NEW YORK • LONDON

ACKNOWLEDGEMENTS

Many people were helpful to the author in providing background information and photographs for use in this book. Special thanks are offered:
David M. Webb, Agricultural Research Service, U. S. Department of
Agriculture; Wade W. McCall, Cooperative Extension Service, University of Hawaii; R. M. Adamson, Department of Agriculture, British Columbia, Canada; S.R. Robins, President, Hydroponics Corporation of
America; George Fielding, Manager, Animal Commissary, Bronx Zoo;
and Tim Sullivan, who posed for many of the photos that appear herein.

CONTENTS

TO MIDGE AND TIM,

WHO KEEP GROWING NICER

1

THE MAGIC GARDENS

Atop a covered-over city dump in Glendale, Arizona, just west of Phoenix, sits a sprawling "food factory," a ten-acre complex made up of hundreds of long, narrow concrete seedbeds, and pipes and pumps, all enclosed within neat rows of fiberglass greenhouses. Each one of the greenhouses covers an area slightly longer than a basketball court and is about half as wide.

The greenhouses are called Magic Gardens. To the more than one thousand visitors who tour the complex each week, the growing process does seem truly magical. For there is no soil here. There are no shovels, hoes, rakes, or other standard items of farm equipment.

Instead of soil, the plants grow in a liquid that provides them with the water and minerals they require. The process is called *hydroponics.**

All the plants are started from seed. Each seedling grows in an individual planting box. When the plants are from

---

*Technical terms used in this book are printed in italics the first time they occur and are defined in the glossary.

Young tomato plants thrive at a hydroponic installation in Arizona. (Jack Sheaffer, *Arizona Daily Star*)

four to five inches in height, they are placed in the concrete growing beds which have been filled almost to the top with shiny gravel.

Three-inch plastic pipes that run parallel to each of the growing beds are the heart of the operation. These pipes carry water and nutrients to the plant roots.

Sensors within the growing beds regulate the valves that control the flow of nutrients through the pipes. Excess solution is drained off and reused.

The growing plants are protected from frost, hail, wind, and insects. There are no weeds, no soil diseases.

Such conditions produce stunning results. Tomato plants,

Mature tomatoes are juicy and flavorful.
(Jack Sheaffer, *Arizona Daily Star*)

climbing on vertical supports, grow to a height of eight or nine feet. The fruit they produce is meaty, juicy, and superb in flavor.

In addition, laboratory analysis has shown that the nutritive value of tomatoes grown hydroponically is higher than that of soil-grown tomatoes.

It's not that the hydroponic process is, by nature, superior to dirt farming. Not at all. Ground-grown tomatoes could equal those produced in the Magic Gardens of Glendale, Arizona, *if* ideal soil conditions could be achieved, and the temperature and humidity as carefully controlled.

Control—that's one of the leading features of soilless cul-

11

**Tomatoes are packed for shipment to local markets.
(Jack Sheaffer, Arizona Daily Star)**

ture. The grower carefully regulates the amount of water the plants receive and both the amount and quality of the mineral foods they require. Also the grower is able to protect the plants from extreme cold and heat and from weather's other ravages.

Because the hydroponic grower has more control over conditions than the soil farmer, results are more uniform. Vegetables are produced on a more predictable time cycle. For flowers, a standard size bloom can be anticipated.

American families may one day use hydroponic growing techniques to produce vegetables for home use. More important, soilless farming promises to help relieve the world's growing food shortage through controllable, expedient methods.

Although the way a plant develops and grows is very complex, it can be explained in simple terms. The most common types of plants have three main parts: roots, stems, and leaves.

Most roots grow underground, supporting the plant as it shoots upward. The roots also absorb the water and minerals the plant needs. In some plants, the roots act to store food which the plant later uses. Beets, carrots, and sweet potatoes are plants with storage-type roots.

**An aerial view of a hydroponic installation.
(Jack Sheaffer, *Arizona Daily Star*)**

Because of the stored food it contains, a sweet potato will produce a healthy vine when suspended in water. Here is a simple experiment.

Pick out the fattest sweet potato you can find.

Stick several toothpicks into the potato and set it on a jar rim. Fill the jar with water so that the potato is about half-covered.

Put the jar in a cool dark place. Keep it there for about ten days, then move it to a sunny window.

Roots will grow from the bottom of the potato and a thick vine will grow from the top.

The roots divide and redivide to form a dense network of rootlets, each one covered with its own root hairs. These fine hairs have cell walls that are *semipermeable,* which means they can absorb water and nutrient elements. This process of absorption is known as *osmosis.*

The stems have several functions. They carry water and minerals from the roots to the leaves. Food is then manufactured in the leaves, and the stems carry this food to other parts of the plants.

The leaves manufacture food by a process called *photosynthesis.* When a plant carries out photosynthesis, a green-colored substance in the leaves called *chlorophyll* absorbs light energy from the sun. The plant uses this energy to make *carbohydrates* from water and minerals (taken in by the roots), and carbon dioxide (taken in by the leaves from the air).

Water, light, air, and certain minerals—these are essential for plant growth. Soil is not essential.

In hydroponic culture, water, light, and air are present. The minerals are simply added to the water in the form of chemical salts. Whether it's a single tomato plant growing in

14

a hydroponic container on a home windowsill, or ten acres of Magic Gardens, the principles are the same.

Soil is a more natural habitat for growing plants than any liquid. Soil provides nutrients and water; it also provides support for the plant through its roots.

But there are vast areas of the world where there is no productive soil, or the soil that is available is too valuable to use for farming. In fact, it has been estimated that only 5 percent of the earth's surface is suitable for conventional agriculture, for dirt farming.

Placed in a water-filled jar, a sweet potato develops attractive vine-like growth.
(George Sullivan)

Hydroponic culture is often used in plant research.
Here a US Department of Agriculture plant physiologist
observes the root system of a soybean plant grown hydroponically.
(US Department of Agriculture)

Flow of nutrients to crops grown hydroponically can be carefully controlled. These are chrysanthemums. (Colorado State University, Department of Horticulture)

This is a woeful statistic when one considers that the world's population is expected to double by the year 2000. Obviously, a world food crisis is at hand.

Hydroponics can help. Hydroponic units can be established by people living in the most barren regions. Urban dwellers, amid all that concrete and asphalt, can grow food hydroponically, too.

The specter of starvation looms for millions of the world's inhabitants. Hydroponics is not going to eliminate that problem. But it might be part of the solution.

17

2

THE HISTORY OF HYDROPONICS

"The chemical gardening idea has recently swept the country from one end to another," proclaimed *Hydroponics* magazine in the spring of 1938. "Garden clubs are hungry and clamoring for enlightenment.

"Many humble homes," the magazine continued, "are growing their own vegetables and enjoying a garden where cramped quarters or impoverished soil previously would not permit such luxury."

Such enthusiasm for soilless gardening was typical of the 1930s. Countless national magazines and Sunday supplements of newspapers featured articles hailing hydroponics as the wonder of the day. It was said that with a few jars and pots and a sprinkling of chemicals, every citizen could turn his backyard into a Garden of Eden.

Such exaggerated claims were bound to lead to disappointment and failure. Before the 1940s has begun, the bubble had burst. It is only in the last few years that hydroponics has begun to emerge from the doldrums.

The first experiments in what is now called hydroponics can be traced to 1699 and John Woodward, a Fellow of the

Royal Society of England. Woodward was successful in cultivating plants in water to which he had added garden soil of different types. He was seeking to determine whether it was the water or the solid particles of soil that sustained plant growth.

In the decades that followed Woodward's research, European plant *physiologists* established many things. They proved that water is absorbed by plant roots, that it passes through the plant's stem system, and that it escapes into the air through pores in the leaves. They showed that plant roots take up minerals from either soil or water, and that leaves draw carbon dioxide from the air. They demonstrated that plant roots also take up oxygen.

The research conducted by two German scientists, Julius von Sachs, a *botanist,* and W. Knop, an *agricultural chemist,* was of particular importance. Knop has been called "the father of water culture." He used the technique to study the basic relationship of soil to crop production. Sachs was more interested in studying plant processes and thus added to botanical knowledge. During the 1860s, they developed solutions that contained the nutrients essential to plant growth and demonstrated that plants were capable of growing to maturity in the solution alone.

By the beginning of the twentieth century, scientists the world over accepted soilless culture as a valid method of growing plants of almost every type. But it was left to Dr. William F. Gericke of the University of California to move hydroponics out of the laboratory and to demonstrate its practical value.

In the late 1920s, Dr. Gericke constructed huge outdoor growing units of concrete. Using a nutrient solution he had

Dr. Gericke inspects potatoes grown hydroponically.
(New York Public Library)

developed himself, and taking advantage of the abundant California sunshine, he produced tomato plants that attained heights of twenty-five feet and over. Picking had to be done from ladders. He also raised many other types of vegetables, as well as flowers, grains, fruits, and several root crops.

It was Dr. Gericke who coined the term "hydroponics," combining the Greek words *hydro,* referring to water, and *ponus,* meaning work. Hydroponics, said Dr. Gericke, meant literally "water working."

"Nutriculture," "chemiculture," and "aquiculture" were other terms used during the 1920s and 1930s to describe soilless culture. No matter what name was used, Dr. Gericke's work showed that soilless culture could be used in the commercial production of vegetables and flowers, that it could be important to agricultural research, and that it could provide a fascinating hobby for the indoor gardener as well.

News of Dr. Gericke's success spread throughout the United States. Many universities established experimental hydroponic units in greenhouses and proceeded to grow such vegetables as tomatoes and cucumbers on a year-round basis.

Soilless culture also enjoyed a brief spurt of popularity among amateur gardeners. But the world of commercial agriculture greeted the reports of Dr. Gericke's experiments with skepticism and, in some cases, outright ridicule. Farmers had not the slightest wish to change methods that had been in use since agriculture began.

Tomato plants grown hydroponically by Dr. Gericke attained stunning size. (New York Public Library)

21

Actually, there are two different types of hydroponic culture, although each is based on the same principle, that of growing plants in a liquid mixture of nutrients instead of in soil.

The difference lies in how the plants are supported. Dr. Gericke's method was to fill shallow tanks with nutrients and cover them with wire mesh. The plant roots descend through the open spaces in the mesh to feed on the solution below. The wire surrounding the spaces holds the plants upright.

The second type of hydroponic culture, used more frequently today, involves the use of some medium to which the plant roots cling, thereby supporting the plant itself. The nutrient solution flows around the particles to get at the roots.

The growing medium is always something *inert,* that is, completely inactive in terms of the growing process. Com-

Dr. Gericke's gladioli were five to six feet in height. (New York Public Library)

22

**Gravel is to be the growing medium in
this hydroponic installation.
(Hydroponics Corporation of America)**

mercial growers frequently use gravel as a medium. Fine
sand, like beach sand, can also be used. So can glass marbles
or stone chips.

The medium is placed in long, narrow concrete troughs
or on plastic sheeting. Plastic pipes with tiny holes are laid on
the surface of the medium near the base of the plants. The
nutrient solution is pumped into the pipes to feed the plant
roots.

23

**Hydroponic tomatoes climb on wire supports in Hawaiian sun.
(University of Hawaii, Cooperative Extension Service)**

Although hydroponics remained in relative obscurity through most of the 1940s, it did find important use in many isolated areas during World War II. The US Air Force and Britain's Royal Air Force set up hydroponic units at remote military bases to grow vegetables that could not be sustained by available soil.

On Wake Island, an atoll in the Pacific Ocean west of Hawaii, the rocky nature of the terrain ruled out conventional farming. The US Air Force constructed hydroponic growing beds there in 1945 that provided 120 square feet of growing area. Once the operation became productive, its weekly yield consisted of thirty pounds of tomatoes, twenty pounds of string beans, forty pounds of sweet corn, and twenty heads of lettuce.

One of the world's largest hydroponic installations was established by the US Army in Chofu, Japan, after World War II. Covering fifty-five acres, it was designed to produce both seedlings and mature vegetables for American occupation forces. It remained in operation until the early 1960s.

The US Army established hydroponic growing beds on the island of Iwo Jima that employed crushed volcanic rock as the growing medium. United States forces on remote Ascension Island in the South Atlantic also learned to grow vegetables hydroponically.

In the past decade, soilless culture has become much more widely accepted than ever before. "Hydroponic farms have proved economical, " *New Scientist* magazine said recently, "in conditions ranging from the burning sandy deserts of Africa and Arabia to the ice-bound wastes of Antarctica, and from the mud huts of Asian villages to the concrete-towered megalopolises of Europe and North America."

Helping to spearhead research and development in the field is the International Working Group on Soilless Culture, with headquarters in the Netherlands. Members represent nineteen countries. The Food and Agricultural Organization of the United Nations is also active in providing advisory and technical information about hydroponics.

Many of the nations of the Middle East now operate hydroponic greenhouses, including Lebanon, Kuwait, and Abu Dhabi. In Abu Dhabi, the installation uses desalted water from the Persian Gulf. Tomatoes and cucumbers have proven to be the most successful crops. Cabbage, radishes, and snap beans have also done well.

A worker tends tomatoes at a hydroponic
installation in Sidney, British Columbia (Canada).
(Canada Department of Agriculture)

The Israelis have been successful in using soilless culture
to farm vast areas of the Negev, a desert region about the
same size as the state of Connecticut in the extreme southern
portion of the country. An unusual technique has been
employed.

The sand is flattened, using a tractor, and is then treated
with fertilizers. Irrigation pipes are brought in and laid in
long rows next to the roots of the plants being grown. Often
sheets of plastic are strung over the crops. Water is precious
in the Negev, and the plastic sheets serve to reduce the
amount of water lost through evaporation. Watering is done
at night for the same reason.

"The soil acts merely to hold the roots," says an Israeli

agricultural expert. "The entire procedure of 'growing' is done by foreign agents acting above the ground."

England is now being supplied with tomatoes grown hydroponically in the Canary Islands. In Holland, Belgium, and several other European countries, hydroponic techniques have been applied to raising flowers, chiefly gladioli and carnations. The Soviet Union has huge complexes of hydroponic farms around Moscow and Kiev.

As for the United States, the most successful hydroponic installations are to be found in Arizona, in Glendale and Tucson. Several acres of hydroponic vegetable beds covered by fiberglass greenhouses are under cultivation in Florida and Utah.

The same is true in Hawaii. Land in Hawaii is so expensive that growers must achieve the greatest possible production from it in order to earn a profit. Some growers have turned to hydroponics as a result. As of 1975, four Hawaiian growers were producing tomatoes hydroponically and more installations were planned.

Louisiana, Texas, California, and Washington are other states where hydroponic installations can be found.

Hydroponics is not used solely by commercial growers. What is known as the *Herbagère* method of hydroponic cultivation, invented by a Belgian botanist named Gaston Perin, is beginning to find widespread use in the United States.

This growing technique utilizes a number of shallow rectangular trays containing *germinating* seeds. The trays are stacked one above the other in a sealed growing chamber. Each of the tray bottoms contains narrow slits. This feature permits nutrient solution introduced at the top tray to drip down through each tray in the stack.

This technique is sometimes referred to as "vertical farming." It has been applied to the growing of highly nutritious grass for feeding to livestock and zoo animals.

The San Diego Zoo is one of a number of zoos that operate a hydroponic growing chamber of this type. It's the size of a large house trailer. Within the chamber, a total of 252 white plastic trays are arranged in several neat tiers.

Each day, thirty-six trays—one-seventh of the total—are seeded with presoaked barley. Nutrient solution is sprayed over the trays several times each day to keep the seeds moist. The temperature within the chamber is kept at from 64° to

Seeding the trays is the first step in vertical farming. (George Sullivan)

In just seven days, seedlings are ready for harvest.
(George Sullivan)

68° F. and the trays are bathed in fluorescent light continuously, which serves to stimulate seed growth.

Since the growing cycle is seven days long, each day mature barley is harvested from another set of thirty-six trays. The *barley* daily harvest yields from five hundred to six hundred pounds of grass and roots. Special trailers whisk the grass to feeding stations throughout the zoo.

Many animals prefer the fresh, succulent barley seedlings to conventional grass. The giant tortoises would rather have hydroponically grown barley than their usual favorite, fresh lettuce leaves. The grass also serves as a substitute for kale.

Zoos in New York City (the Bronx Zoo), Chicago, and Phoenix operate the same kind of growing chambers. At the Bronx Zoo, the grass is fed to most of the hoofed stock—the zebra, antelope, deer, and Mongolian wild horses.

Lettuce is another crop that lends itself to vertical farm-

At the Bronx Zoo in New York, Mongolian wild horses
feast on the fresh, succulent seedlings.
(George Sullivan)

ing. Lettuce seedlings in inch-and-a-half planting boxes are
placed in trays which are stacked one above the other in
metal racks. After a twenty-eight-day diet of liquid nutrients, the plants reach maturity.

The lettuce is marketed with the original planting box still
attached. Watering the box keeps the lettuce fresh and crisp
in the refrigerator for a period of up to three weeks.

3

PROS AND CONS

All of this should not imply that hydroponics is the perfect growing system. It represents only one element of the many that influence plant growth. Light, temperature, and humidity are some of the others. In soilless culture, just as in dirt farming, each one of these factors must be taken into consideration.

But the system does offer some clear-cut advantages. For one thing, hydroponics makes for a more efficient use of land being cultivated. In the case of tomatoes, the dirt farmer raises about 3,500 plants per acre. But in hydroponic culture, the plants can be placed much closer together. It's possible to cultivate as many as 10,000 plants on an acre of land. Cucumbers and beans are other crops in which the plant population per acre can be significantly increased over dirt farming.

In normal farming, crops have to be rotated, that is, grown in a fixed order of succession. A crop of green beans may follow one of tomatoes; alfalfa may follow lettuce, etc. Otherwise, the nutrient level of the soil falls below established minimums. Plainly speaking, the soil "wears out."

**Many more plants per acre is one advantage
of hydroponic culture.** *(Arizona Daily Star)*

With soilless culture, there's never any need to rotate
crops. The "farmer" checks the solution constantly and adds
whatever nutrients may be needed. Thus the nutrient level
can be just as high at harvesttime as it was the day the crop
was planted, and the same type of crop can be grown in
endless succession.

If, however, the grower decides he wants to change to a different crop after the harvest, it's a simple matter to do so. Generally speaking, leaf crops thrive on a solution that stresses *nitrogen,* while root crops prefer an emphasis on *phosphorus.* With soilless culture, all the grower has to do is alter the nutrient solution to accommodate the particular needs of the crop to be cultivated.

With soilless culture, the back-breaking task of weeding is eliminated. You never see a rake or hoe or any type of cultivator on a farm that utilizes hydroponic growing methods. Once in a while a random windblown weed seed may manage to get a start in the gravel, but weeds are never a major problem, nor even a minor one.

Growing does not have to be done on a seasonal basis, either. The fact that conditions of heat and humidity can be controlled permits the grower to operate twelve months a year. He can harvest tomatoes on New Year's Day, if he wants to. All he has to do is plan the growing cycle accordingly.

This fact could have important impact on farm-labor conditions. The problem now is that almost all farm work is seasonal, with the grower's need for labor lasting no more than four or five months. But in the case of soilless culture, there is a need for workers on a year-round basis. Workers involved in hydroponic culture can thus enjoy the same advantages in terms of salaries and other benefits as do factory workers or office workers.

Of course, there are also some disadvantages.

When soilless culture is attempted on a commercial basis, plant disease can be a serious problem. When the agent causing the disease is present in the circulating solution, every plant in the growing unit can be struck down in a matter of hours. Scientists have yet to develop any counter-agent that can be dissolved in the solution to control disease while the crop is growing.

Growers do all they possibly can to check the outbreak of disease. When the growing beds are not in use, powerful chemicals are circulated through the pipes, beds, and growing medium to sterilize them.

Determining the amount and type of nutrients takes much knowledge and experience. (University of Hawaii, Cooperative Extension Service)

The high cost of setting up a hydroponic operatic is another drawback. The concrete growing beds must be on-structed, and the pipes and pumps necessary to carry the nutrient solution to the plants must be installed.

If the operation happens to be in a part of the world where frost or subfreezing temperatures can be expected, the growing beds have to be enclosed within a greenhouse type of structure, and provisions then have to be made for heat and humidity control. Compare all of this to dirt farming, where about the only essential requirement is a piece of land.

With commercial hydroponics, there is also the matter of technical knowledge. As the plants feed in the nutrient solution, they change its chemical makeup. Fresh nutrients have to be added to replace those used. Analyzing the solution requires a laboratory, and specialists to staff it.

Despite these shortcomings, hydroponics represents the most logical method of growing a wide range of vegetable crops in areas of the world where good soil is in short supply.

Some scientists foresee huge towerlike hydroponic farms within major cities. Green vegetables, fresh and inexpensive, would be available on the spot every day of the year.

Plans are being drawn for using the techniques of soilless culture on space flights and even on the moon. For hydro-ponics, the future seems very bright.

4

THE TOOLS OF
HYDROPONICS

Soilless culture can be applied to the growing of many handsome foliage plants. Ten such plants are listed on pages 45 through 47.

NUTRIENTS

These plants do not need special feeding. What food they do require is obtained from the sun and water. But with the addition of *nutrients,* they will grow faster and be more healthy.

While you can make your own nutrient solution (following the instructions given in Chapter 8), it is much easier to use one of the powder or liquid plant foods available in garden shops, florist shops, or even supermarkets. All you have to do is follow the directions on the package label. In almost every case, the label explains how the product can be adapted for use in soilless gardening.

If the label fails to give specific instructions covering water culture, then cut the amount that is recommended by one-half. Always keep in mind that it is better to underfeed than overfeed.

Some garden-supply companies manufacture and sell premixed chemicals especially for use in connection with hydroponic growing. These firms are listed in the appendix at the end of this book.

One of these products is Hyponex, described as a scientifically compounded mixture of chemicals in dry form which, when dissolved in water, yields a nutrient solution that supplies all the elements necessary for vigorous plant growth. To make a nutrient solution from Hyponex, simply mix one or two level teaspoons of the powder with a gallon of water.

Store the solution in an opaque container. Plastic gallon jugs, the kind that contain household bleach, are ideal. Be sure to wash the container thoroughly.

Commercial plant foods are not expensive. A ten-ounce package of Hyponex costs about one dollar; a five-pound package, about five dollars. One pound of the powder makes one hundred gallons of solution.

WATER

The chances are very good that the tap water in your home will not present any problem. However, if you live in an urban area, you may have to be concerned about the amount of chlorine the water contains. Chlorine is a chemical that is added to water to purify it. Too much chlorine will retard the growth of plants. But there is a simple way to solve the problem. Fill a crock or other large vessel with water and let it stand for a day or two. The chlorine will work its way out.

You can also get some idea of the quality of the water you're planning to use with this simple test: Place a few cut

Plastic containers like this are excellent for storing solution. (George Sullivan)

flowers in a glassful of water and let them stand for a day or two. If the flowers show no ill effects, presume the water will be satisfactory for soilless culture.

Don't hesitate about using water from the hot-water tap. Most indoor gardeners avoid it as if it were impure. Not at all. Simply let it stand until it cools to room teperature before you use it. Water from the hot-water tap is likely to be the chemical equivalent of cold water that has been allowed to stand for some time. In the process of heating, some of the chlorine is drawn off.

Avoid using water softened by a home appliance. Water softeners change the water's chemical makeup. While the result may mean plenty of suds in the bathtub, the plants do not enjoy it.

Depending upon where you live, you may also have to be

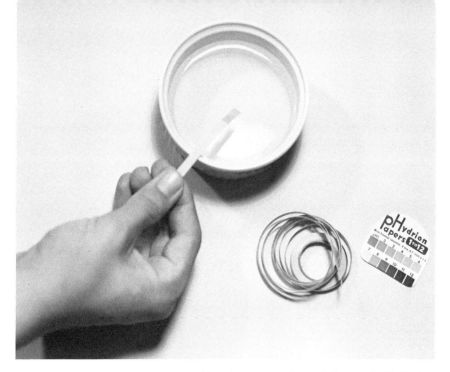

**Testing water for acidity and alkalinity.
(George Sullivan)**

concerned about the acidity or alkalinity of your water. In the eastern United States, limestone deposits are sometimes to be found on the sloping terrain of the watersheds, and these cause the water to have a high alkaline content.

To check water for acidity or alkalinity, purchase a pH measuring tape at a garden center or chemical-supply store. Or perhaps your science teacher in school has one that you can borrow. The letters pH stand for p(otential) H(ydrogen).

Snip off a two- or three-inch length of pH tape and dip it in the water. Then watch what color the tape turns. Should the tape become orange, it indicates a pH reading of 5, which is quite acid. Deep green or blue indicate readings of 10 or 11, that is, high alkalinity. Most plants prefer water that has a pH reading of between 6 and 7.

If you find your water is too alkaline, collect a gallon in a clean container and add a few drops of vinegar. Test again with the pH strip. By a trial and error process, you'll arrive at the right mixture.

If the water is too acid, add a few drops of a solution of bicarbonate of soda, commonly known as baking soda. Then test again.

CONTAINERS

Besides water and a nutrient, about the only other thing you need is a container in which to grow the plant. You can use any type of container made of glass, porcelain, or other ceramic material. Avoid copper, brass, or lead containers. When filled with water and plant nutrients, these often generate chemicals that can be harmful to plant life.

Purchase your plants at a garden-supply store or florist shop. They don't need to be very big. Plants in two-inch or three-inch pots do nicely.

Be imaginative in your choice of containers. Use mason jars or small fishbowls. Use laboratory beakers, flasks, or even test tubes.

Be aware, however, that clear glass containers, when filled with water and allowed to stand in sunlight, give rise to a filmy green layer of aquatic plant life known as *algae.* When allowed to grow uncontrolled, the algae will slow the growth of your plant by using up the oxygen in the water. You can, however, cover the sides of the vessel with opaque paper or aluminum foil to keep the light out of a clear glass container.

You can also retard the growth of algae by using tinted glass containers. The darker the glass, the fewer the algae. If you use an opaque container, algae will never be a problem.

There's a wide range of containers from which to choose.

But there's a drawback to using a nontransparent container. You can't see the roots develop, and often what goes on underwater is just as exciting as what happens on top. It's for this reason that clear glass containers are preferred by most people.

If you decide on clear glass, change the water and rinse off the plant roots when the algae forms. You'll probably have to do this about once a month, depending on how much sunlight the plant receives.

GROWING MEDIUM

Many of the plants that you can grow indoors in a nutrient solution need some type of inert material so the roots can anchor themselves and support the plant.

Gravel is the best material of this type. The term *gravel*

41

usually refers to small rock fragments or chips. But in hydroponics, gravel means small pebbles, like those found in the bed of a fast-running stream.

The size of the gravel is important. If the pebbles are too small, oxygen won't be able to circulate among them. If they're too big the roots won't be able to cling to them. Ideal size for the pebbles is between one-quarter inch and three-eighths inch in diameter.

Gravel can be purchased at a garden-supply store. Or maybe you can gather some from a stream bed or ocean beach. In the case of beach pebbles, be sure to give them a thorough rinsing to remove the ocean salt.

If you want to experiment, you can use any one of a number of other inert materials. Sawdust, wood chips or shavings, scraps of foam plastic, chips of broken dishware or phonograph records—any of these can serve as the growing medium. But gravel is the best.

5

HYDROPONICS
AT HOME

There are many plants that will thrive indoors. All you really need is tap water and a sunny window. No soil. Not even nutrients.

Cut half-inch slices from the tops of carrots and beets. (Be sure the leaves have been removed.) Arrange five or six on a saucer. Add water to the depth of one-quarter of an inch. Keep the water at this level. Put the dish in a sunny place. Within a day or two, the carrots will begin to produce delicate ferny tops. The beets will send up dark green leaves with veins of deep maroon.

The top of a pineapple will grow into a thick-leaved plant. Cut a two-inch section from the top of the pineapple. Remove the leaves. Put the top in a dish and add water. Keep the dish in a sunny window. In a few weeks, roots and leaves will begin to form.

Plants that grow from bulbs are ideal for soilless culture. Try hyacinth bulbs or narcissus bulbs, available at a garden-supply store. You'll have best results if you pick out bulbs that are already showing a bit of green at the top.

Above, Kept supplied with water,
carrot tops sprout quickly.
(George Sullivan)

Left, The hyacinth is
easy to grow.
(George Sullivan)

Cover the bottom of a deep dish with a two-inch layer of pebbles. Anchor three or four bulbs in the pebbles, pointed ends up. Fill the dish with water so that it just touches the bottom of the bulbs. Place the dish in a cool, dark place. Plan to leave it there about a month.

Check the water level from time to time. If you let the dish go dry, the bulbs might die. On the other hand, too much water can cause the bulbs to rot. When the dish has become filled with roots, move it to a sunny window.

Following is a list of plants which, with a reasonable amount of care, will flourish in water (or in water and nutrients) indoors. The common names are given first, then the scientific names.

Arrowhead plant (*Syngonium podophyllum*)—This plant derives its name from its arrowhead-shaped leaves. It's sold not only in garden shops but in variety stores and some supermarkets. As this implies, it's one of the simplest plants to grow. Arrowhead plants like to climb, and you can provide them with twine supports. Or you can cut back the new growth. Either way, the plant thrives.

Chinese evergreen (*Aglaonema medestum*)—Another very easy plant to grow indoors, the Chinese evergreen is also one of the handsomest. It has dark green shiny leaves, somewhat oval in shape, and a thick main stem. Curiously, the plant is also known as the Japanese evergreen.

Coleus (*Coleus blumei*)—This is among the most showy of all houseplants, its leaves marked with red, yellow, or white. Sometimes the plant is called painted nettle. Coleus requires direct sun to attain its best color. Cut back new shoots to encourage bushy growth.

Dwarf umbrella plant (*Cyperus alternifolius gracilis*)—Large

45

The arrowhead plant
is appropriately named.
(George Sullivan)

Planting the Hawaiian ti log is a cinch.
(George Sullivan)

umbrella plants shoot to the ceiling, but this variety won't grow beyond twelve or fourteen inches in height. Umbrella plants like warmth and some shade.

English ivy (*Hedera helix*)—This is only one of the dozens of varieties of ivy that thrive indoors. Some are climbers; others are creepers.

Hawaiian ti (*Cordyline terminalis*)—When purchased, this plant often has the appearance of a short length of corn stalk. There's no soil, no pot; it comes packaged in a small plastic envelope. Often it's to be found in gift shops where it's sold as a novelty item. Long, narrow green leaves, sometimes edged in pink, grow from the plant's central stem. Hawaiians used to use the foliage for thatching their roofs and making hula skirts.

Japanese sweet flag (*Acorus gramineus*)—A handsome plant that grows a thick clump of swordlike leaves, the Japanese sweet flag fares best in a partially shaded window.

Philodendron (*Philodendron oxycardium*)—"Unfailing"— that's the word for the philodendron. It's to indoor gardening what scrambled eggs are to the amateur cook. The philodendron will tolerate conditions of light that would quickly eliminate other plants. It will thrive on plain water. Cuttings root quickly. The plant will creep or climb—as you wish. If you have any doubts as to your gardening skill, buy the philodendron.

Ribbon plant (*Dracaena sanderiana*)—One of the several tropical plants of the dracaena (*dra-see-na*) family, this plant gets its name from its shiny leaves, gaily striped in deep green and white. Like all dracaenae, it's a fast grower.

Wandering Jew (*Zebrina pendula*)—A native of tropical America, this is a fast-growing creeper with deep green

Ornamental cup makes an attractive container for this philodendron. (George Sullivan)

and purplish leaves. If given moderate warmth and sun, it will produce small, three-petaled flowers.

If the plant comes in a pot with soil or potting mixture, carefully remove it in the following manner. First, wet the soil thoroughly. Turn the pot upside down. Holding your palm over the open end of the pot, with the plant stem between two fingers, gently tap the pot edge against the

Gravel helps keep this ribbon plant upright. (George Sullivan)

Zebrina—wandering Jew—is gaily striped. (George Sullivan)

To remove the plant, invert the pot, tap it gently.

edge of a table. The plant and the soil should slide free in one clump.

Remove excess soil particles. Then soak the plant roots in a pan of lukewarm water to remove the remaining soil. Be careful in handling the plant roots; they're easy to damage.

Fill the new growing container with plain water. When you put the plant in the container, the water should cover the roots and part of the stem.

After a few days, pour out the plain water and replace it with nutrient solution. As the solution level drops because of evaporation, add plain water. Don't add more nutrient solution; doing so will cause too great a concentration of the chemical salts.

After rinsing the soil from the roots, put the plant in the new growing container.

**A teaspoon of powdered charcoal will keep
the container and gravel sweet smelling.
(George Sullivan)**

If the plant is too small for the container and won't stay upright, place a few glass marbles on the container bottom and nest the plant roots or stalks among them. Or you can use aquarium gravel, which can be purchased at a pet shop or the pet counter of a variety store.

If you use support material of this type, you should also add a pinch of powdered charcoal to the water. This can be purchased at a garden-supply store or perhaps a pet shop. Charcoal helps to keep the water and support material sweet smelling.

It's important that the plant roots be supplied with oxygen from time to time. One way to accomplish this is to replace

51

the water in which the plant is standing with fresh water. Or, if you're using a nutrient solution, replace it with solution from a new batch. Plan to do this at least once a month.

You can also pump oxygen bubbles down to the roots by means of a rubber household syringe. On each squeeze, get the nozzle as close as you can to the roots.

A bicycle pump is still another method of providing the roots with oxygen. If you use this method, be sure to remove the pump nozzle from the water on every "up" motion of the handle. A minute of pumping should be sufficient.

A watering can is pretty much of a necessity, especially if you're going to be caring for several plants. The containers lose water constantly through evaporation. In a hot, dry room, you may be surprised how quickly water levels go down.

Get a plastic watering can with a long spout. It should not cost any more than a dollar or two. This type will enable you to pour without spilling, even in the case of a hard-to-reach container.

Using soilless culture, you can also grow many types of flowering plants indoors. However, in order to develop and grow, decorative plants require much more light than foliage plants. Before you decide what species of plant you wish to grow, be sure to make an evaluation of the amount of light available. This subject is discussed in Chapter 6.

A bush rose will do nicely in a large jar filled with nutrient solution. Choose a variety of rose that's not going to climb. Consider one of the many varieties of dwarf roses, some of which grow no more than twelve or fourteen inches in height.

Following the directions given earlier in this chapter, rinse the soil or peat moss from the plant roots. Use lukewarm water. Be very gentle in handling the roots.

Fill a one- or two-quart glass jar with nutrient solution to within about three inches of the jar rim. Suspend the plant roots in the solution. Do not permit the root crown, that part of the plant between the roots and the stem, to become submerged.

To keep the plant standing upright, pack cotton in the space between the stem and the inside of the jar rim. Don't

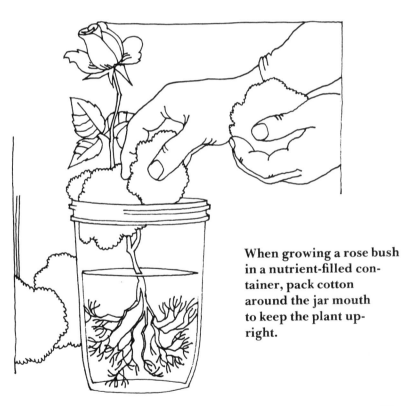

When growing a rose bush in a nutrient-filled container, pack cotton around the jar mouth to keep the plant upright.

pack the cotton too tightly, however. Air must be able to flow through the cotton to the exposed roots.

As the plant begins to develop, you'll notice that the most root growth occurs in the two- or three-inch air space between the cotton and the surface of the nutrient solution. From time to time, you can aerate the deeper roots by removing the cotton and spurting bubbles into the solution with a rubber household syringe.

Keep the solution at the original level; otherwise, too much of the root system may become exposed. This will probably mean that you will have to add some solution each day to replace that used by the plant and lost through evaporation. Of course, how frequently you add solution depends upon the size of the plant and the conditions of temperature and humidity.

Every two weeks, empty out the solution and replace it with solution from a new batch. Do it quickly; if the roots dry out at all, the rose's health is in danger.

Most flowering plants, including those mentioned toward the end of this chapter, require a container with a wide opening. A flowerpot, the size depending on the plant, serves nicely. You can also use bowls, crocks, cookie jars, or bean pots. Just be sure the container is glass, a type of porcelain or stoneware, or plastic. Never use a metal container.

Prepare the container by covering the bottom with a thin layer of gravel. Add a tablespoon or two of powdered charcoal.

Holding the plant so that the roots are just touching the gravel, add more gravel until it reaches the stem. Fill the container half-full with plain water.

In a few days, replace the plain water with nutrient solution. Again, only fill the container halfway.

Left, Use gravel
of this size.
(George Sullivan)

Below, Add gravel
until it reaches
the stem.

55

The upper and lower halves of the container serve as two separate growing chambers. The lower half contains the nutrient solution, supplying the plant with the water and minerals it needs. From the upper half, the plant derives its oxygen.

Check the solution daily. When the level drops through plant use and evaporation, add more water. The gravel should be thoroughly but slightly damp at all times.

About once a month, give the gravel a thorough rinsing. First, empty the container of all solution. Fill it with plain water, then pour it out. Do this two or three times, then add fresh solution.

Chrysanthemums are one of the countless types of flowering plants that quickly adapt to gravel culture. There are hundreds, perhaps thousands, of varieties of chrysanthemums. Choose a variety that appeals to you for its color, the particular time of year that it blooms, either summer or fall, and one that is suited to the amount of growing space you have. If it's limited, select a bushy, short-stemmed variety.

The African violet has long been a particular favorite of indoor gardeners. Characterized by lush foilage and, depending on the variety, purple, pink, or white flowers, the plant thrives in gravel and nutrients. Its botanical name is *Saintpaulia.*

The *begonia* is another flowering plant you may wish to try. Several books have been written on the begonia, a plant native to the tropics. Its leaves are often brightly colored or heavily veined. Its waxy flowers come in many colors.

Bromeliads are another large family, most members of which do well indoors. Spanish moss, the zebra plant, and the pineapple are bromeliads.

The begonia is one type of flowering plant you
can grow hydroponically. (George Sullivan)

Bromeliads are of many different types.
(Duro-Test Corporation)

Growers of bromeliads, begonias, and African violets have their own organizations to exchange ideas and information. If you decide to specialize in the growing of any one of these plants, you may wish to become an organization member. Addresses of these organizations are listed in the appendix.

6

PLANT CARE

Although "magic" and even "miraculous" are words some-times used in connection with hydroponics, this shouldn't imply that plants growing in a nutrient solution will always prosper on their own. The truth is that the success of each individual plant is pretty much related to the amount of care and concern it receives.

Foliage plants usually do require as much maintenance as flowering plants. But all plants require almost daily supervision in order to assure maximum growth and development.

Light is the most important single fact in growing plants indoors successfully. A plant may exist and look healthy for an extended period in a location where the light level is low, but its growth will be seriously retarded. If the light level remains poor, the plant will eventually weaken and die.

Many factors influence the amount of light that passes through a window. The size of the window, for one thing, and whether it has curtains, shades, or blinds that screen out the light.

Obstructions can also be on the outside—trees or tall buildings.

The direction in which the window faces is a critical matter. An east or west window admits significantly more light than a north window.

Finally, the distance the plant is going to be placed from the window has to be considered. The closer, the better.

Many *horticulturists,* people who specialize in cultivating plants, especially for ornamental use, classify conditions of light as being low, medium, good, or direct.

The best light is direct light. This means that the direct rays of the sun fall on the plant at least three or four hours on a sunny day. If you are fortunate enough to have direct light, you will be able to grow with ease any plant mentioned in this book.

Good light is derived when a plant is placed directly in front of an unobstructed east or west window, or a partially obstructed south window.

Medium light is produced when a plant is placed directly in front of an obstructed east or west window or directly in front of an unobstructed north window. You also get medium light when the plant is placed a few feet from or to either side of an unobstructed east or west window.

Low light conditions result when the plant is placed directly in front of an obstructed north window. They are also derived when the plant is placed to either side of an unobstructed north window, or when it is placed up to ten feet from or to either side of an unobstructed east or west window.

To determine how much light a plant requires, you should consider how it grows in its natural habitat. For example, the Chinese evergreen, the ribbon plant, and the philodendron (plants mentioned in Chapter 5) grow in thick tropical forests and are heavily shaded. Thus, they are able to grow indoors in low light. Other foliage plants mentioned in Chapter 5 require no more than medium light.

Generally speaking, the more exotic a plant, the more light it requires. The African violet and begonia need light that is from medium to good. As for bromeliads, many species are easily grown, but some require light conditions that are at least good.

If your window light in your home is not sufficient for the plants you wish to grow, you can supplement it with artificial light.

Incandescent light bulbs are an adequate source of artificial light, providing the light shines directly onto the foliage. Incandescents specially manufactured for indoor gardeners range in size from sixty to five hundred watts. Reflectors are built into such bulbs to give them a spotlight effect.

One problem with incandescents is the heat they generate. Even though the plants you are growing may be tropical plants, they will not enjoy intense heat.

When the surface of the leaves reaches a temperature of 85° F., a plant is no longer able to photosynthesize. Photosynthesis is the process by which the cells in green plants convert light into food that sustains the plant and produces new growth. Even in the tropics, plants carry out photosynthesis only when leaf temperatures are below 85° F.

If the leaf surfaces of a plant feel warm to the touch, chances are the leaf temperatures are above 85° F. In such a case, move the light farther away.

Opposite, **This planter features artificial light.**
(Courtesy GTE Sylvania Incorporated)

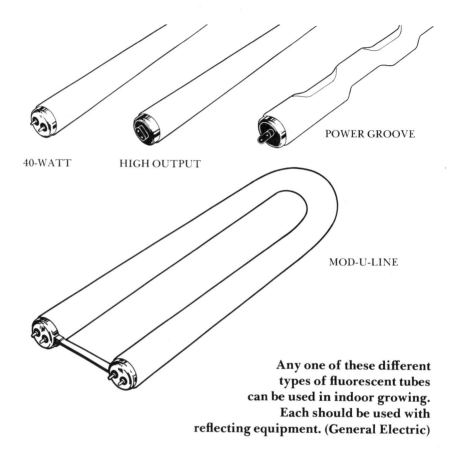

40-WATT　　　HIGH OUTPUT　　　POWER GROOVE

MOD-U-LINE

**Any one of these different
types of fluorescent tubes
can be used in indoor growing.
Each should be used with
reflecting equipment. (General Electric)**

Fluorescent tubes are the best source of artificial light for indoor gardening. They consume a relatively small amount of electricity for the amount of light they produce. And because the heat output is spread over such a large area, the problem of heat is sharply reduced.

You can purchase a fluorescent unit for your plants that includes the tubes themselves, reflectors, and a stand. You place the unit on a table or shelf and plug it in. That's all there is to it.

The type of fixture, the number of tubes you require, and their size depend on the kinds of plants you're growing and the amount of window light you already have. Two lamps thirty-four inches in length should provide about medium light, even in a dark room. To improve conditions, simply increase the number or size of the tubes.

There is much more to the topic of gardening under artificial light than this book can cover. If you're planning to do much gardening without sunlight, or without sufficient sunlight, you should consult one of the many books on the subject (see Further Reading in the appendix).

The right amount of humidity is also important to plant development. It can become a critical problem in dry climates or in the wintertime, when windows are closed and home heating dries the atmosphere.

Moisture in the atmosphere is expressed in terms of *relative humidity.* In the average home, the relative humidity usually ranges from 40 to 55 percent. When it falls below 40 percent, as it might do during the winter, the health of some plants become endangered.

You can keep track of the humidity in a room by an instrument known as a *hygrometer.* It registers relative humidity by means of a semicircular dial, or by a column of mercury, the way a thermometer registers temperature readings. A hygrometer costs from ten to thirty dollars. If you buy one, hang it on a wall close to your plants, but not so near that it will be wetted by any spraying you might do.

One way to raise the humidity of a room is to set out an open pan of water. You can also correct conditions of low humidity with a humidifier. This is usually an electrically powered unit which disperses a fine mist into the air, drawing upon a reservoir that contains several gallons of water. But such a unit is expensive. A better and cheaper way to provide your plants with the humidity they need is by misting.

The most successful indoor gardeners mist their plants daily. Misting is different from spraying and requires a misting can or mister that will deposit a thin coat of droplets on the plant surfaces. It does no good to drench the foliage.

Misting can do more than just freshen your plants. If you include nutrients in the water, you will also be feeding them.

**A misting can.
(George Sullivan)**

Another benefit of daily misting is that it helps to keep the foliage clean. Leaves that become dust covered deny the plant the light it needs. You can buy a misting can at almost any garden-supply store for about $3.50.

If you don't mist your plants, then you should sponge the leaves from time to time to keep them clean. Use warm water and a mild soap, being sure the solution is well diluted.

The temperature of the room is not likely to cause you any problems. Most types of plants do well in temperatures ranging from 60° F. to 80° F. Tropical plants do their best in temperatures between 70° F. and 90° F. But almost all plants can tolerate temperatures below or above these minimums and maximums. This does not mean, of course, that they can be subjected to freezing temperatures or stifling heat.

It's not likely that your plants will be bothered by insect pests, but should they be, the problem is not difficult to solve. Summer is the time to keep a sharp lookout for insects.

White flies are one type of pest that may infect your plants. These are tiny white insects that fly about when plant leaves are disturbed. The white fly lays its eggs on the undersides of leaves. Hatchings occur at intervals, so any treatment you follow must be continued for a good while.

While white flies are tiny, mites are even tinier. Some gardeners keep a magnifying glass close at hand in order to be able to spot them.

There are many different types of mites, but all live on the undersides of leaves where they spend much of their time spinning webs. While you must closely examine the leaves to find the mites, the webs will tell you that they are there.

Either mites or white flies are capable of killing a plant if allowed to remain unchecked. As soon as you become aware of the presence of one of these insects, begin eradicating them. But stay away from commercial pesticides. Using pesticides indoors, whether powder, liquid, or aerosol spray, is dangerous because of the lack of ventilation. Don't think that just because you hold your breath or close your eyes as you treat the plant that you're going to be safe. The chemical can linger in the air for days, and its harmful effects may not manifest themselves for weeks or even months.

To rid a plant of either white flies or mites, all you need to do is wash the leaves. Make a strong solution from brown laundry soap and a pail of lukewarm water. Add a tablespoon of household ammonia.

Wash each leaf carefully, then give the plant a good rinsing using a fine spray. Do this every two or three days for about three weeks.

You have to be thorough; you have to be persistent. But the method always works.

It's a good idea to keep a careful record documenting the care each one of your plants receives. Begin the record with a notation of the date you received the plant and how you obtained it.

Make a notation whenever you feed the plant. This entry should mention the amount of nutrient solution added and its makeup. Later, jot down what results were achieved— new leaves, root development, or budding.

If you move a plant from one location to another, record the effects of the changes in light and temperature. Make an entry whenever you wash the foliage.

Hydroponics is far from being an exact science. Indeed, there are many aspects of soilless culture on which horticulturists disagree. Some scientists say that direct sunlight on

Use mild soap solution when washing plants.
(George Sullivan)

the roots is harmful to root growth; others say it's beneficial. Whether the water or solution should be changed frequently is another point that's being argued.

Keeping a record of your observations is the best way there is to build your store of knowledge about the field. Your journal will also help you solve problems as they arise and reduce or eliminate errors.

7

GROWING VEGETABLES FROM SEED

Seeds, like mature plants, require water, oxygen, and light to grow. They do not require soil.

Try this experiment: Take some grass seed and sprinkle it on a damp sponge. Place the sponge in a sunny window. Keep it damp.

Germination will occur within a few days. After the seeds absorb sufficient water, the outer skins will burst and the tiny embryo plants begin growing. The young roots will force their way downward, anchoring themselves to the sponge. The pointed stems will shoot upward toward the light.

All of this happens because the seeds have been provided with the essentials of growth: water, oxygen, and light.

The seedlings will continue to grow until they have used all of the food stored in the seed. Then they will weaken and die. But if the seedlings are fed regularly with a nutrient, they will develop into mature plants.

To grow vegetable seedlings hydroponically, you can use just about any type of container, so long as it gives you six or seven inches of depth. A ceramic planter or large flowerpot, either clay or plastic, will do nicely.

If you want to raise several different types of seedlings all at one time, use a fiberglass window box, the type available at garden-supply stores. One that is thirty-six inches long, six inches wide, and six inches deep costs about four dollars.

As a nutrient solution, use a commercial powder or liquid. Simply follow the mixing instructions on the package label.

Growing seedlings hydroponically requires the use of special growing media such as *vermiculite* or *perlite*. Vermiculite is produced from *mica*. Mica is a mineral that occurs in nature in crystalline sheets that press together like pages in a book.

Sprinkled in a damp sponge, grass seeds sprout quickly. (George Sullivan)

Vermiculite has a spongy feel.
(George Sullivan)

Once mined, the mica is milled and screened, then placed in a furnace and subjected to temperatures of about 2,000°F. The water within the mica turns to steam, expanding the original particles to twelve times their normal size. These particles are soft, delicate, absorbent, and very light in weight. When the tiny particles are examined closely, they are seen to curl slightly, giving them a wormlike appearance. The term *vermiculite* is from the Latin word *vermiculus*, meaning "small worm." A cubic foot of vermiculite weighs only a few ounces.

Most vermiculite is used as an insulating material by the building and engineering trades. Only a relatively small amount finds use as a growing medium.

You can purchase vermiculite in almost any garden-supply store. It is often sold under any one of an assortment of trade names. It costs about twenty-five cents a quart. Look for particles that are silvery in color and smaller than gravel chips in size. The kind used by builders takes the form of large, flat chips which are soft to the touch. This type isn't recommended for growing plants from seeds. Because the vermiculite is usually bagged in clear plastic, it is easy to see what you're buying.

In the process by which vermiculite is produced, oxygen becomes trapped within the tiny particles. This provides another advantage to the seedling grower; plant roots are able to feed on this oxygen.

Vermiculite is clean; indeed, it is sterile. It is easy to handle. To commercial growers, however, vermiculite has several disadvantages. In time, the air cells within the particles collapse, and the material packs together, forming lumps or even a solid mass. No oxygen can get to the plant roots as a result. Another problem arises in any attempt to sterilize the vermiculite with liquid chemicals. This is relatively a simple matter when gravel is being used, but the vermiculite absorbs the chemicals, thereby ruining itself as a growing medium. But these shortcomings apply only to the commercial operator seeking to grow mature crops. For raising seedlings hydroponically in containers of any type, vermiculite is highly recommended.

Perlite, another inert material often used in soilless mixes, has many of the same characteristics as vermiculite. It is a porous natural volcanic glass, often called sponge rock. Not only does it retain water, but like vermiculite it also provides oxygen for the plant roots.

One problem with perlite is that it's buoyant, and some particles rise to the surface when watering is done. Some gardeners reject perlite because it does not have a natural look, being light gray and looking like a plastic.

Should you decide to use perlite and purchase a package, notice that it contains a fair amount of perlite dust. Get rid of the dust. It can only cause problems. Perlite costs about twice as much as vermiculite.

No matter what variety of vegetable or flower you're planting, be sure to get the best seed you can buy. The difference in price between good seed and poor seed is slight, but the difference in results can be enormous.

It's best to buy from a seedsman or garden-supply store rather than from a supermarket or variety store. No matter where you buy, check the date stamp on the packet to be sure that the seed is intended for the forthcoming season.

Within the last decade or so, the use of coated seed has become fairly widespread. The coating contains nutritional materials and also serves to protect the seed from certain diseases and from rotting. In addition, it makes the seed easier to handle. Coated seed is well suited for soilless culture.

Begin by covering the bottom of your container—whether it be a flowerpot or a window box—with a half-inch layer of drainage stones. Use gravel or small rock chips.

Over the drainage stones, add sufficient vermiculite to fill the container to within three-fourths inch of the top.

The next step is to water the vermiculite. At this stage, use

74

plain water, not nutrient solution. Simply sprinkle on water until the vermiculite is wet throughout. The surface should be only as moist as a wrung-out sponge.

Many novice gardeners make the mistake of sowing seeds too deeply. A good rule of thumb to follow is to plant seeds four times as deep as their diameter. (In the case of seeds you've purchased, follow the instructions on the seed packet.)

If you're planting a window box, use the sharp end of a pencil to make two parallel trenches over the length of the box. The depth of the trenches depends on the size of the seeds. Seldom will they be deeper than one-fourth inch.

Sprinkle the seeds into the trenches. The bigger the seeds, the more growing room each requires. Then cover the trenches.

Spray the surface enough to moisten it. Do not firm down the vermiculite with your hand.

If you're sowing seeds in a flowerpot, simply scatter them at random over the surface of the vermiculite. Then sprinkle a thin layer of dry vermiculite over them. The final step is to give the surface a very light spraying.

The seeds might begin germinating within a few days, or it might take as long as a week or two. It depends on the type of seeds you've sown. The first stages of growth will be tiny shoots, called *plumules,* that appear above the surface.

Keep in mind that there is enough food material within the seeds to sustain this first growth. Nutrients aren't necessary yet. All you need to do is keep the vermiculite damp.

Too much water is as bad as too little, however. If the seeds become soggy they can die from a lack of oxygen. Keep the soil as moist as a wrung-out sponge.

Tomato seedlings flourish in vermiculite.
(George Sullivan)

As soon as the first growth is apparent, begin thinning. Pull out enough plants so that those that remain aren't crowded.

Begin the use of nutrients after the seedlings are an inch or so in height and have grown their first true leaves. True leaves are the second pair of leaves that form.

How often you apply the nutrient solution depends on many things. The size of the container in which the seedlings are being grown and the stage of growth that the plants have attained are factors that must be considered. Leafy plants, such as lettuce and beets, require more nutrients than nonleafy ones.

In the summer, it may be necessary to apply solution every other day. If the plants show signs of *wilt,* more frequent applications are probably necessary. In the winter, one or two applications a week may be sufficient.

When the seedlings are three or four inches in height, you can begin transplanting them. Use a teaspoon to remove each plant, being very careful not to damage the tender roots. Take as much vermiculite with the plant roots as the teaspoon can hold.

There are many types of vegetables that you can grow to maturity using soilless-culture techniques. However, don't attempt to grow vegetables indoors unless you have direct light (see Chapter 6). Even outdoors, most kinds of vegetables require three or four hours of midday sun.

Tomatoes are more widely grown among both amateur and commercial hydroponicists than any other type of vegetable.

There are many varieties of tomatoes to choose from. If you're going to be growing the plants indoors, select a red-cherry or red-plum type. These plants are smaller than most of the other varieites, and thus much less troublesome to stake and support. In addition, the fruit matures faster.

You can grow germinated tomato seedlings to maturity in an individual flowerpot, or plant several in a fiberglass window box. A window box that is eight inches deep and thirty-six inches in length can accommodate three or four tomato plants, depending on the variety.

If the window box has no provision for draining off excess solution or water, drill four drainage holes in the bottom of the box. They should be one-fourth inch in diameter. Keep them well spaced. Plug the holes from the outside with cork stoppers. (See diagram on page 79.)

Use gravel as the growing medium. Cover the bottom of the pot or box with a six-inch layer of gravel. As the tomatoes begin to mature, you will have to use some type of litter

**Red cherry tomatoes
are a good variety
to grow indoors.
(Burpee Seeds)**

to support the growing plant and provide it with an area in which roots can develop. Wood shavings or excelsior make excellent litter. Either one holds the plant upright and permits air to circulate freely.

When you transplant, first rinse the vermiculite from the plant roots, then set the roots in the gravel. Place litter around the plant to hold it upright. Plan on spraying the litter with nutrient solution frequently to keep it moist.

As the plant develops, remove one-half to one inch of gravel, replacing it with more litter. Roots will develop on the litter level and grow down into the gravel to feed on the nutrient solution.

Keep enough solution in the container so that the roots in the gravel are entirely covered. When the temperature is high, or evaporation rapid, or both, you may have to add

78

solution every day. No matter what, never let the roots dry out.

Every two weeks flush out the gravel with plain water. Remove the drainage plugs and let any excess solution drain out. Don't try to reuse it. Then add water, letting it drain through the gravel and seep out through the drainage holes. Do this two or three times. This washes out the impurities that have begun to accumulate. The process should take only a few minutes.

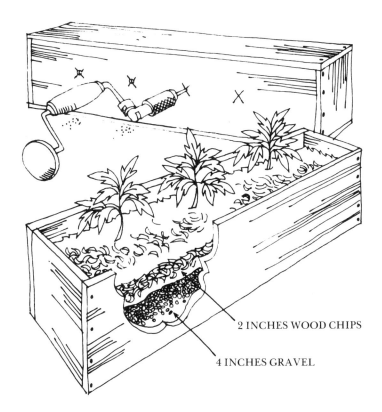

2 INCHES WOOD CHIPS

4 INCHES GRAVEL

For drainage, drill holes in the container bottom.
Use wood chips or excelsior to keep the plants upright.

When you have finished flushing out the gravel, replace the cork stoppers. Add fresh solution from a new batch.

Each plant must be pruned as it grows, that is, the unproductive side shoots must be removed. The more pruning you do, the more quickly fruit matures, but the total crop will be smaller.

If you're growing tomatoes, the plants have to be *pollinated*. Grains of *pollen* must be carried to the *pistils* of the flowers to fertilize them. Tomato plants are easy to pollinate. Simply shake the plants gently when the flowers are in bloom. In the case of plants grown outdoors, the wind does the pollinating. How long it takes the tomatoes to grow to maturity depends on the variety. Some produce fruit in sixty-five to seventy days.

In the experiments he conducted in soilless culture at the University of California in the 1920s and 1930s, Dr. William F. Gericke demonstrated how to grow a tomato plant hydroponically in a one-gallon glass jug.

He would fill the jug with nutrient solution to within an inch or so of the neck. He mounted the plant seedling in a small cork and packed cotton around the cork to hold it in place within the jar neck. He then adjusted the solution level so that the seedling's roots were entirely covered.

When the plant was about two feet high and the roots had grown about eight inches down into the solution, he dropped the solution level three or four inches. This permitted more oxygen to get to the plant roots and contributed toward a healthier, faster-growing plant.

Other vegetables you can grow hydroponically are beans, beets, and lettuce. These are easier to grow than tomatoes

Snap beans
can be grown
indoors, too.
(Burpee Seeds)

because there is no need to first germinate the seed in vermiculite. It can be started directly in the main growing unit.

To grow snap beans, lima beans, or French green beans, use gravel as the growing medium. If you're going to be growing the beans indoors, take care in making your selection, because some varieties produce stems that are eight to ten feet tall. Choose bush beans or dwarf varieties.

Plant the seeds about one inch deep. It takes seven to nine days for the seeds to germinate.

Thin the seedlings so that the plants are five to six inches apart. When the plants are in bloom, shake each one gently to pollinate the flowers.

Sow lettuce and beet seeds in sand and grow the vegetables to maturity in it. Don't use seashore sand or the packaged material sold in garden stores as sandy soil. Instead, use builders' sand. Wash it several times in plain water before you plant the seeds.

In the case of lettuce, germination takes six to eight days. Thin the seedlings until the growing plants are six inches apart.

It takes from forty-five to ninety days for the plants to reach maturity. Keep this in mind when selecting your seed, and pick out a variety that will mature quickly.

You're likely to have much more success with leaf lettuce than head lettuce. Leaf lettuce has large, loose, frilled leaves which spread out as the plant develops.

While lettuce requires a more frequent application of solution than most plants, it's important not to allow the roots to become waterlogged. This causes the lower leaves to wither and die. Merely keep the sand moist.

Beet seeds take eight to ten days to germinate. Keep the plants spaced three or four inches apart. Some varieties reach maturity within sixty days. Don't forget that the leaves can be eaten as well as the roots. In fact, some gardeners grow beets just for the tops, harvesting the plants before the beets themselves have reached maturity.

A number of firms (listed in the appendix) sell hydroponic growers for home use. One type has a growing bed about the size of a small window box. Perlite, used as the growing medium, and a supply of liquid nutrients in concentrated form are included with the unit.

Once mixed, the solution is stored in a tank beneath the growing bed. With a flip of a switch, the solution is pumped

You're likely to have better results with leaf lettuce than head lettuce. (Burpee Seeds)

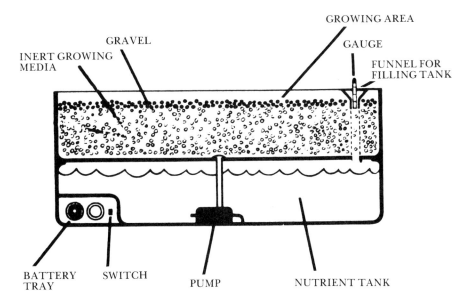

INERT GROWING MEDIA

GRAVEL

GROWING AREA

GAUGE

FUNNEL FOR FILLING TANK

BATTERY TRAY

SWITCH

PUMP

NUTRIENT TANK

**This hydroponic grower is battery powered.
(Hydroponics Corporation of America)**

through the perlite. It takes only a minute or two, with small batteries providing the pump's power.

Some home units are equipped with fluorescent light fixtures to supplement window light. Commercial hydroponic growers of this type begin in price at about forty dollars.

During the early 1970s, hydroponic greenhouses became available for backyard use. A unit with floor space that measures ten feet by twelve feet costs about $1,500. Larger and more elaborate units cost three and four times that amount. Such greenhouses are equipped with growing trays or beds and the pumps and pipes necessary to keep the beds supplied with nutrient solution.

The owner of a small hydroponic greenhouse is said to be able to produce all the fresh vegetables needed by a family of four or five, provided he operates the unit on a year-round basis. By 1975, more than five hundred hydroponic greenhouses were in operation in the United States.

83

8

MIXING YOUR OWN NUTRIENTS

You may wish to mix your own nutrient solution, particularly if you're doing any large-scale growing.

Another advantage is one of control. For example, a lack of growth and development can be caused by a deficiency in nitrogen. Should a plant appear stunted, you might want to increase the amount of nitrogen it's getting. This is an easy matter if you're mixing your own nutrient solution.

This chapter gives two solution recipes. Others are presented in the bulletins and books listed in the appendix.

The ingredients can be purchased in a pharmacy, although you might have to shop around to obtain them all. They are also available from chemical-supply companies.

Be careful in measuring out the ingredients. Too great an amount of any one of the salts mentioned below can seriously damage your plants. In hydroponics, remember, there is no soil to absorb excess amounts of salts or chemicals. You're applying them directly to the roots.

Be certain to use glass, ceramic, or plastic containers when doing your mixing. Metal can cause unwanted chemical reactions.

Store the solution in an opaque container. The plastic gallon jugs that contain household bleach are excellent. Just be sure to wash them thoroughly.

Scientists divide plant mineral requirements into two groups; major and minor, called "bulk" and "trace." The trace elements are just as important as the bulk elements. It's simply that they are not required in such large amounts.

The bulk elements include hydrogen and oxygen, which the plants obtain from the water, and carbon, taken in as carbon dioxide from the air.

There are six other bulk elements the plants take up from the soil or, in the case of soilless culture, from the nutrient solution. They are: *nitrogen, phosphorus, potassium, calcium, sulfur,* and *magnesium.*

Each has its own function. Nitrogen produces lush green growth. Without it, the plant turns yellow and its growth is retarded.

Phosphorus is essential to the plant cells and, thus, important in many of the plant's vital activities. Should there be a lack of phosphorus, the cells will fail to develop normally.

Potassium is necessary for many of the chemical reactions that take place within the plant. It is concentrated wherever there is growth activity, such as in the development of the leaves or flowers.

Calcium is essential for the formation of cell walls. Sulfur, distributed throughout the plant in small amounts, is present in certain plant proteins. Magnesium is necessary for the formation of chlorophyll.

Chemical salts that provide each of these bulk elements are used in preparing nutrient solutions. One tried and proven formula for preparing one gallon of solution is as follows:

Potassium nitrate [KNO_3]	4 grams
Magnesium sulfate [$MgSO_4$]	4 grams
Potassium phosphate [K_2HPO_4]	4 grams
Calcium nitrate [$Ca(NO_3)_2$]	4 grams

Dissolve each one of the salts in a separate pint of water. If you're using tap water that you think might contain chlorine, allow it to stand for several days to allow the chlorine to evaporate. Label each jar with the name of the salt.

To prepare the nutrient solution, pour the jars of dissolved salts one by one into a one-gallon container, stirring the mixture as you pour. It's important to mix in the salt solutions in the order they're listed above—first, potassium nitrate; second, magnesium sulfate, etc. This assures that the salts will remain in solution.

After the four pints of salt solution have been poured into the gallon container, add two more quarts of plain water to give you a full gallon. Store the solution in an opaque container.

To each gallon of the salt solution you must add twenty drops of the trace element solution. Here are the ingredients needed to make one pint of trace solution:

Boric acid [H_3BO_3]	1.0 gram
Manganous sulfate [$MnSO_4$]	0.5 gram
Zinc sulfate [$ZnSO_4$]	0.5 gram
Copper sulfate [$CuSO_4$]	0.5 gram
Sodium molybdate [$NaMoO_4$]	0.2 gram
Iron tartrate	2.0 gram

Dissolve each one of these chemicals separately in an ounce of water. Mix them in the order listed, the boric acid first, then the manganous sulfate, and so on, stirring as you mix.

Add enough water to make one pint. Store the trace solution in an opaque container. It will keep for several months.

A second nutrient solution recipe is easier to prepare. The chief ingredient is commercial fertilizer, the type you can buy at a garden-supply store. The type of fertilizer to buy is described as 8-8-8. You can also use 8-8-10. These fertilizers do not contain magnesium or iron. But you can supply these with the addition of Epsom salts and sulfate of potash.

Dissolve one pound of 8-8-8 (or 8-8-10) fertilizer, three ounces of Epsom salts, and two ounces of sulfate of potash in a gallon of tap water. This becomes your stock solution. It is *not* to be applied directly to the plants but is used in making nutrient solution. Store the stock solution in an opaque container.

To prepare the nutrient solution, mix one ounce of stock solution into a gallon of tap water. This, too, should be stored in an opaque container.

Plants themselves provide the best evidence as to whether they are getting a balanced diet. For example, when a plant needs more nitrogen, its leaves are undersized, and its growth in general is stunted. In the case of a serious nitrogen deficiency, the leaves turn yellow and die.

A deficiency in magnesium also causes a stunted appearance. The leaves, except for their veins, turn yellow and become shriveled.

If a plant does not get enough phosphorus, the edges of the leaves begin to yellow, and the leaves at the bottom of the plant drop off. A lack of potassium is indicated when the leaves become mottled or have a scorched look and the leaves' edges turn yellow, then brown.

When calcium is lacking in the plant's diet, growth stops. Leaves at the top of the plant turn yellow and die.

A deficiency of iron can also cause a yellowing of the leaves at the top of the plant. Also, there is likely to be a yellowing of the other leaves from the edges inward. The stem takes on a bleached appearance. These things happen because iron is closely linked to the formation of chlorophyll. Once iron is restored to the plant's diet, the leaves quickly regain their greenness. An iron deficiency can also slow the plant's rate of growth.

Insufficient sulfur is difficult to perceive because it does not show until late in the growth period. The roots do not develop properly and the plant fails to attain normal size.

Watch for such evidence. Whenever your plants show signs of one type or another of deficiency, adjust the solution accordingly. And though your experiments may be limited to a single container, you are in fact duplicating the techniques used by commercial hydroponic growers.

APPENDIX

FOR FURTHER READING

Books

BENTLEY, MAXWELL. *Commercial Hydroponics Facts and Figures.* Johannesburg, South Africa: Bendon Books, 1959.

BRIDWELL, RAYMOND. *Hydroponic Gardening.* Santa Barbara, California: Woodbridge Press Publishing Co., 1974.

DOUGLAS, JAMES SHOLTO. *Beginner's Guide to Hydroponics.* New York: Drake Publishers, Inc., 1972.

GERICKE, W.F. *The Complete Guide to Soilless Gardening.* New York: Prentice-Hall & Co., 1940.

HARRIS, DUDLEY. *Hydroponics: Gardening Without Soil.* Capetown, South Africa: Purnell & Sons, 1966.

LOEWER, PETER. *The Indoor Water Gardener's How-To Handbook.* New York: Popular Library, 1973.

MCDONALD, ELVIN. *The Complete Book of Gardening Under Lights.* New York: Popular Library, 1973.

TICQUET, C. E. *Successful Gardening Without Soil.* New York: Chemical Publishing Co., 1956.

Bulletins

GROWING CROPS WITHOUT SOIL. US Department of Agriculture, Agricultural Research Service, Beltsville, Maryland, 1970.

GROWING PLANTS WITHOUT SOIL. Circular 440, Cooperative Extension Service, University of Hawaii, Honolulu, Hawaii.

HYDROPONIC CULTURE OF VEGETABLE CROPS. Circular 192, Florida Agricultural Extension Service, University of Florida, Gainesville, Florida, 1966.

HYDROPONICS. Department of Horticulture, Colorado State University Experiment Station, Fort Collins, Colorado, 1974.

HYDROPONICS AS A HOBBY; GROWING PLANTS WITHOUT SOIL. Circular 844, University of Illinois, College of Agriculture, Extension Service in Agriculture and Home Economics, Urbana, Illinois, 1962.

HYDROPONICS: THE SCIENCE OF GROWING PLANTS WITHOUT SOIL. Bulletin 180, Florida State Department of Agriculture, Tallahassee, Florida, 1958.

METHODS OF GROWING PLANTS IN SOLUTIONS AND SAND CULTURES. Bulletin 636, New Jersey Agricultural Experimental Station.

A SUCCESSFUL HYDROPONIC GARDEN FOR WARM CLIMATES. Soils Department, University of Florida, Gainesville, Florida.

MANUFACTURERS OF PLANT NUTRIENTS

Hydroponic Chemical Company, Inc. (Hyponex)
Copley, Ohio 44321

Schultz Company (Schultz-Instant Liquid Plant Food)
11730 Northline Boulevard
St. Louis, Missouri 63040

Hydroponics Corporation of America (Vitalizer)
745 Fifth Avenue
New York, New York 10022

Hydroponics Company (Super-Gro)
PO Box 3215
Little Rock, Arkansas 72201

J. M. McConkey Co., Inc.
PO Box 309
Sumner, Washington 98390

Sierra Chemical Co.
PO Box 275
Newark, California 94560

SEEDSMEN

Herbst Brothers Seedsmen, Inc.
100 North Main Street.
Brewster, New York 10509

Vaughan-Jacklin Corp.
5300 Katrine Avenue
Downers Grove, Illinois 60515

W. Atlee Burpee Co.
Doylestown, Pennsylvania 18901

George W. Park Seed Co.
Greenwood, South Carolina 29646

WINDOWSILL GROWING UNITS

Hydroponics Corporation of
  America
745 Fifth Avenue
New York, New York 10022

Burwell Geoponics Corporation
Box 1235
Rancho Sante Fe, California 92067

HYDROPONIC GREENHOUSES

Hydroculture, Inc.
10014 West Glendale Avenue
Glendale, Arizona 85301

PLANT SOCIETIES

African Violet Society of America
603 East Essex Avenue
St. Louis, Missouri 63122

Bromeliad Society
1811 Edgecliff Drive
Los Angeles, California 90026

American Begonia Society
10331 South Colima Road
Whittier, California 90604

GLOSSARY

AGRICULTURAL CHEMISTRY—The study of how certain elements and compounds affect the life processes of plants

ALGAE—Any one of the numerous primitive chlorophyll-containing plants that occur in fresh or salt water

BEGONIA—Any of the family of tropical plants, widely cultivated as house plants

BOTANY—The science of plants and plant life

BROMELIADS—Various plants of a family which includes pineapple, Spanish moss, and many species grown as houseplants

CALCIUM (Ca)—A chemical element that plants derive from nutrient solution (or the soil) and that is necessary for the development of cell walls

CARBOHYDRATE—Any of a group of chemical compounds, including sugars and starches, made up of carbon, hydrogen, and oxygen

CHLOROPHYLL—The green color-ing matter of plants essential to the production of carbohydrates

EMBRYO—An organism in the early stages of development; in the case of a plant, before sprouting

GERMINATE—To start growing or developing

GRAVEL—Loose rounded fragments of rock; small pebbles

HERBAGÈRE—A method of hydroponic cultivation in which rectangular, slitted trays containing germinating seeds are stacked one above the other within a growing chamber. Nutrient solution is permitted to drip from the top of the stack to the bottom through each tray

HORTICULTURIST—A specialist in the cultivation of plants, especially those for ornamental use

HYDROPONICIST—A specialist in soilless plant culture

HYDROPONICS—The cultivation of

plants in water containing dissolved nutrients, instead of in soil

HYGROMETER—An instrument that measures relative humidity

INERT—Lacking the power to move; inactive

MAGNESIUM (Mg)—A chemical element taken in by the roots that the plant uses in the formation of chlorophyll

MICA—A mineral that splits into thin, partly transparent layers

NITROGEN (N)—A chemical element that occurs as a gas in various minerals and in all proteins; helps produce green growth in plants

NUTRIENT—A substance or ingredient which furnishes nourishment

OSMOSIS—The absorption of fluids through the membranes of root hairs

PERLITE—A natural volcanic glass which, in heat-expanded form, is used in soilless mixes

PHOSPHORUS (P)—A chemical element taken in by the plant roots that is vital to cellular growth

PHOTOSYNTHESIS—The process in which green plants utilize light energy from the sun to manufacture carbohydrates and carbon dioxide

PHYSIOLOGIST—A scientist who specializes in the study of the essential life processes and functions

PISTIL—The seed-bearing part of a flower

PLUMULES—Tiny shoots, the first stage of growth of a plant

POLLEN—The fine, yellowish powder which, when carried to the pistils of flowers, fertilizes them

POLLINATE—To transfer pollen in the process of fertilization

POTASSIUM (K)—A chemical element taken in by the plant roots that is necessary for strong growth

RELATIVE HUMIDITY—The amount of water vapor in the air, expressed as a percentage of the maximum amount of vapor that the air could hold at a given temperature

SEMIPERMEABLE—Partially able to be penetrated by water or nutrients

SULFUR (S)—A chemical element taken in by the roots, which occurs in small amounts throughout the plant

VERMICULITE—Mica in a greatly expanded state; used in soilless mixes

WILT—To become limp; droop

INDEX

94